# THE KIDS' BOOK OF
# CHESS

# THE KIDS' BOOK OF
# CHESS

BY HARVEY KIDDER

ILLUSTRATIONS BY KIMBERLY BULCKEN ROOT

WORKMAN PUBLISHING · NEW YORK

*To my son, David—*

*A liberally educated person
is one whose mind works well
in all areas. . . . Chess should
certainly be part of his education.*

Copyright © 1970, 1990 by Harvey Kidder

Illustrations © 1990 by Workman Publishing

**Library of Congress Cataloging-in-Publication Data**

Kidder, Harvey.
Kids' book of chess and kids' chess set / by Harvey Kidder.
p.   cm.
Rev. ed. of: Illustrated chess for children. 1970.
Summary: Traces the history of chess, describes the pieces and how they move, and discusses the strategy of the game.
ISBN 0-89480-767-6
1. Chess—juvenile literature.   [1. Chess,]   I. Kidder, Harvey.
Illustrated chess for children.   II. Title.   III. Title: Kids' book of chess.
GV1446.K5     1990
794.1'2—dc20                                     89-40787
                                                 CIP
                                                 AC

Workman books are available at special discounts when purchased in bulk for premiums and sales promotions as well as for fund-raising or educational use. Special editions or book excerpts can also be created to specification. For details, contact the Special Sales Director at the address below.

Workman Publishing Company
708 Broadway
New York, NY 10003

First Printing August 1990
10   9   8   7   6

# Contents

Part

# 1 What Is Chess?

magine yourself as a general, *with an army to command!* And the object of the campaign? *To capture the enemy King!*

Opposite you is another army and another general—and the better leader will win! Exciting?

This is the game of chess—the oldest and greatest skill game ever invented.

A chess army is much the same as our army today. It is made up of many types of soldiers and all types of people.

Not all the soldiers in chess or in real life are professional soldiers. In fact most are amateurs—civilians—as we will learn.

Just as people in real life are different, the pieces on the chessboard do not look alike or move in the same way. However, once we think of them as real people, we will always remember how they move.

The game of chess was first played many centuries ago in China, India, and Persia.

Then, in the eighth century, armies of Arabs known as Moors overran

*Armed from head to foot, the knight is ready for battle.*

Persia. The Moors learned chess from the Persians and brought the game with them when they invaded Spain.

From Spain chess quickly spread throughout all of Europe.

The Europeans gave chess pieces the names we know today, which are **Castle, Knight, Bishop, King, Queen,** and **Pawn.**

They probably had trouble pronouncing and spelling the Persian names, so they modernized them to reflect the way they lived.

Today the names don't sound very modern, but imagine for a moment that we were living a thousand years ago.

From a *castle* window we might see serfs, or *pawns*, at work in the fields; perhaps a *knight* approaching in his glittering armor, or a *bishop* leaving a nearby church;

■ *The name "chess" comes from the Persian* shah, *which means "king."* □

and the *king* and *queen* might even grace the scene.

No doubt in those days the names seemed up-to-date and ordinary—much the same as our speaking of the corner drugstore or the local policeman.

The six different chess pieces represent a cross section of medieval life. The way they look, where they are placed on the chessboard, the ways in which they move and even their names all relate to our picture of medieval life with its pomp, pageantry, and conflict.

Now let's talk about the pieces, and who and what they stand for.

*Pawn*

*Castle*

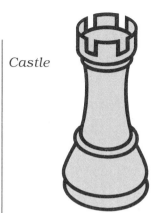

*Knight*

We start with the **Pawns.** They are the serfs, the laborers, the poor. And as in any society, there are more of them than anyone else.

Each side has eight Pawns.

They are the foot soldiers. Often they must be lost in order to protect the more valuable pieces.

But they can also press the attack, inflict crushing losses, and even end the battle by trapping the King!

A Pawn may also be promoted on the field of battle during a game, much the same as any foot soldier today.

The **Castle** is the fort, the refuge, the home. He is easily identified for he looks exactly as he should.

Each side has two Castles.

A castle tower served as lookout.

The **Knight** is the only professional soldier. (Remember, we said that the chess army was a civilian one.) Knights fought on horseback, carrying long, steel-tipped spears called lances.

In that era people did not travel very much. A person might live a lifetime without going more than thirty miles from his birthplace.

The knights, however, were a different breed. They sought adventure, often traveling thousands of miles during the Crusades.

There are two Knights on each side.

*Bishop*

*Queen*

*King*

This is the **Bishop**, who represents the Church.

The Church was very much a part of everyone's life in medieval times. When we learn how the pieces move we will find how well the Bishop and the Castle work together. Church and home—a strong combination!

There are two Bishops on each side.

The **Queen** is next. She is the only woman on the board, and the most powerful piece. Later we'll see that her moves combine both that of the home (Castle) and that of the Church (Bishop). Woman, home, and Church—the most powerful combination on the board!

Perhaps you've heard the phrase "the power behind the throne"? Nowhere is this more true than in the game of chess.

Each side has but one Queen.

And here is the **King**—royalty—the unquestioned authority, the tallest piece on the board.

The king was well defended by his subjects, for his surrender would mean the loss of the kingdom.

This is true in chess, also. If you do not protect your King, you lose the game!

Obviously he is the *most important*—but not the most powerful—piece on the board.

There is but one King on each side.

Now as we look at a set of chess pieces, we can imagine them as a cross section of the people who lived a thousand years ago, from the most powerful to the very poor.

■ *The term "free lance" comes from medieval times. It describes a Knight who was free to carry his lance (in other words to fight) for anyone who paid him.*

# Part 2

# How the Chess Pieces Move

irst let's look at the chess-board—the battlefield. It is square in shape, with thirty-two dark and thirty-two light squares. The board is always put down with a light square in the lower right-hand corner (as you face the board).

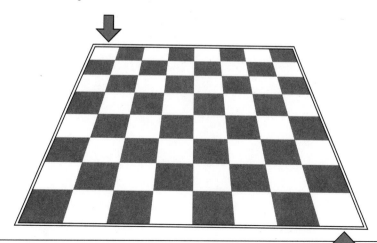

*The chess pieces represent a cross section of medieval life.*

The chess pieces move in a number of ways.

One way is *up and down:* dark square to light square to dark to light, etc., toward your opponent's end of the board and back. Or *from side to side:* dark to light to dark to light, etc.

This is called moving **on the square.**

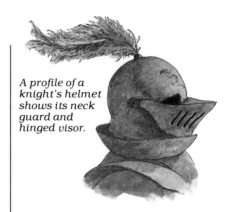

*A profile of a knight's helmet shows its neck guard and hinged visor.*

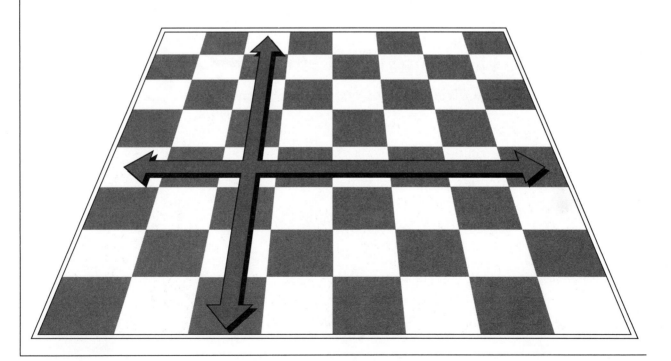

# HOW THE CHESS PIECES MOVE

But there is another way to move, *from corner to corner.* This is called moving **on the diagonal.**

On the diagonal move, you cross the corner of one square into the corner of the next, always through squares of the same shade, either light or dark. This move is never made through both light and dark squares.

Later, we will see how different chess pieces use the square and the diagonal to make their moves.

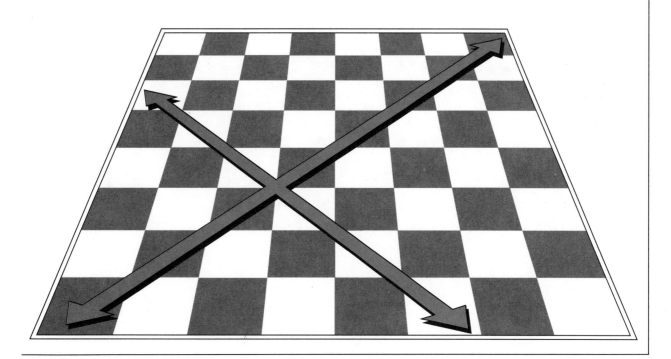

Let's think of the chess-board as a great field of battle, and the chess pieces as two armies of equal strength facing each other. Each army has sixteen pieces.

This is the way the pieces are set up at the start of the game.

Now we'll set them up, piece by piece.

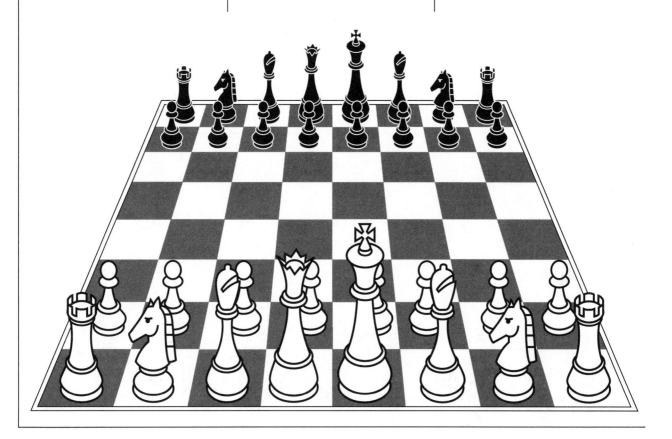

# H O W   T H E   C H E S S   P I E C E S   M O V E

Across the back of the board (or field of battle, if you like) are placed the more powerful pieces. The fortress-like ones, called Castles, are placed in the corners, like this.

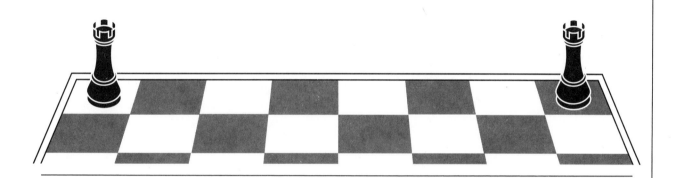

Next to them are the Knights, represented by the horses they ride into battle.

Now come the Bishops, whose Church was next in importance to royalty. In chess, too, the Bishops' position is next to the King and Queen.

This leaves two empty squares in the center of the row. They are for the King and Queen. But which way do they go?

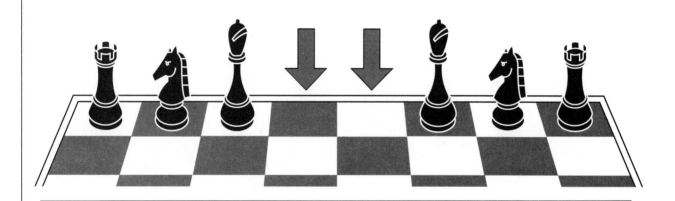

Here we have to remember a little phrase: "Queen on her color." The Black Queen goes on the black square.

Like this.

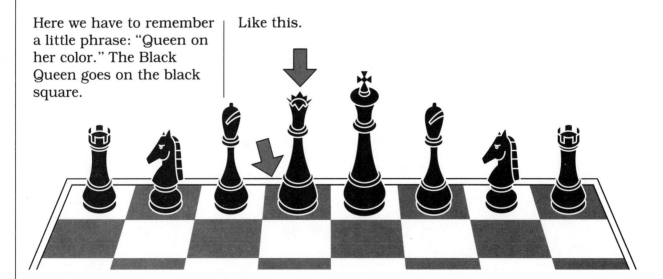

Now we have placed the important and powerful pieces.

In front of each is placed a Pawn.

They are the foot soldiers, so naturally they're in the front lines.

The other side (White) is set up exactly the same, again with the "Queen on her color."

Now let's bring out your chess set, setting up the pieces as we have learned,

so that we can actually move them.

Ready to begin?

# The Pawn

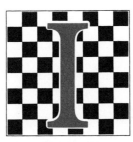**I**magine the chess Pawn in real life, traveling on foot and carrying a long spear called a pike. On the battlefield he was known as a pikeman.

Pikemen also carried shields, which they held directly in front of them for protection. This meant that they had to point their pikes to either side of the shield.

Similarly, because of his shield, a chess Pawn is unable to strike an enemy piece in the square directly in front of him. He can attack only on the diagonal.

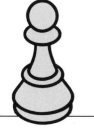

*With their shields before them, pikemen march into battle.*

So we can now see how the Pawn moves:

**1** The Pawn moves forward, one square at a time.

**2** Pawns can never move sideways and can never back up. When two enemy Pawns meet in the same row, neither one can move.

**3** Pawns take or capture only to the forward diagonal square, either to the right or to the left.

Then, having removed an enemy piece from the board and taken his place, the Pawn continues to move straight ahead in the new row.

**4** On the first move only, each Pawn can move out two squares (if the player wishes). After that, the Pawn can move only one square at a time.

This unusual move no doubt reflects the real-life situation when the pike-man felt a little bit more reckless with his army so close behind him. Later he became cautious and took but one step at a time.

■ *Unlike the other chess pieces, the Pawn can never move backward.* □

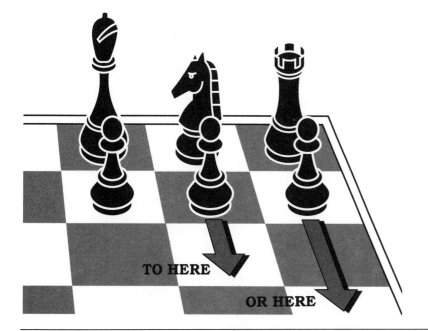

TO HERE

OR HERE

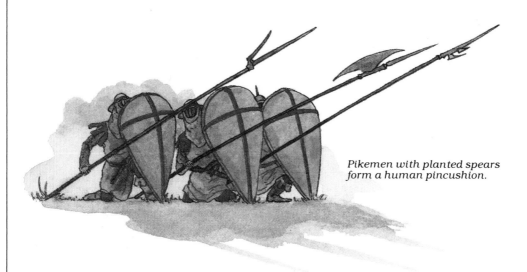

*Pikemen with planted spears form a human pincushion.*

The Pawn does not seem very powerful, but he can be very important later in the game. If he can fight his way to the opposite end of the board, he can be promoted—and become any other piece, even a Queen! (Of course, never a King.) No other chess piece can be promoted to a higher rank. Because they can become powerful, Pawns should be protected by other Pawns or by stronger pieces.

Fighting side by side, the pikemen developed a tactic in battle to stop enemy horsemen. They drove the blunt end of their pikes into the ground and crouched behind their shields, together forming a sort of human pincushion.

Imagine what would happen if a knight should charge!

In the same way our chess Pawns, when properly placed in a game, form a protective wall.

# HOW THE CHESS PIECES MOVE

Below is an example of how Pawns back up each other. Let's call them 1, 2, 3, and 4 and place them on the board like this. Remember that the Pawn captures *on the diagonal*, always moving diagonally onto a square of the same color.

In our chess battle formation, if Pawn number 3 is attacked, either 2 or 4 can destroy the attacker and move up into the position originally held by 3. In a fight among Pawns there might be a fairly even exchange (Pawn for Pawn), but Pawns are also able to destroy any other piece and can even force the King to surrender!

The terms **attack, strike,** and **capture** all mean the taking of an enemy piece.

When you attack, you do not jump over an enemy piece. You merely move into the square he occupies and remove him from the board. Your chess piece stands exactly where the enemy's piece once stood.

■ *Note that the Pawn's attack differs from his move.* □

# The Castle

t is easy to think of a castle as being built of great square blocks of stone with a corner-stone. And logically enough the chess Castles are placed in the corners of the board.

Again, the Castle itself with its huge blocks of stone makes you think of the carpenter and the mason. Their tool, of course, is the square. And that is exactly how the Castle moves—*on the square.*

*A bowman takes aim from the security of the castle—the medieval fort, refuge and home.*

The Castle moves *up and down* or *from side to side*—as many squares as he wishes. This means he can do two things the Pawn cannot. He can move backward and sideways, but he cannot move on the diagonal.

*The king and queen made the castle their home.*

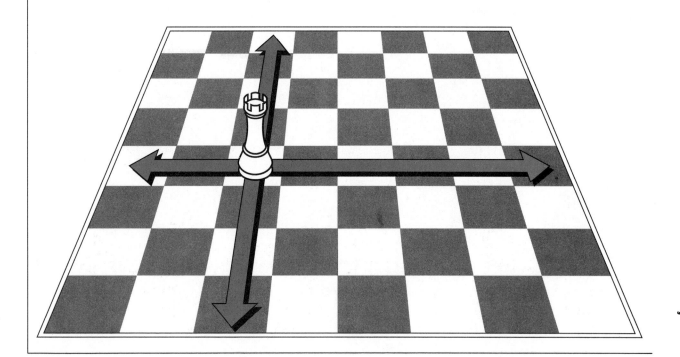

# HOW THE CHESS PIECES MOVE

As you play chess, you'll hear the words "rank" and "file." Both are military terms and both are used to explain chess moves.

**Rank** refers to a row of soldiers, side by side, such as the Pawns at the beginning of a game.

**File** might be thought of as a single file, or column, of soldiers, moving forward or backward.

The Castle can sweep across any open rank or file.

The Castle can capture any enemy piece that is in the direct path of his rank or file.

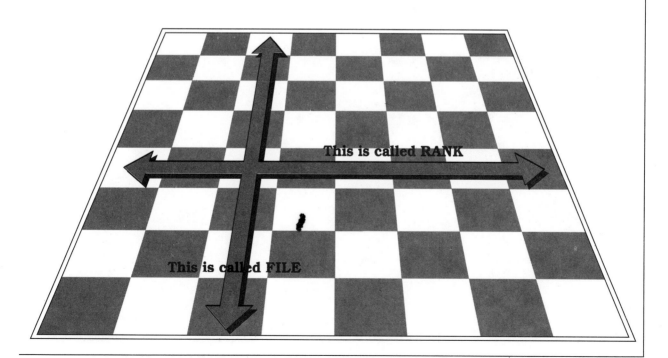

In the illustration below, the Castle can attack any of three Pawns. However, one of these attempts would be a most dangerous move.

Do you see which one? And why?

You are the White player.

How would you move your Castle?

The answer is on the opposite page.

**Answer:** The Castle could strike either Pawn number 1 or Pawn number 4 without endangering himself. If he were to attack Pawn number 2, however, he himself would be captured by Pawn number 3!

Notice how Pawn number 3 backs up Pawn number 2.

■ *The Castle is also known as the "Rook." In fact, most chess players call it by that name. But to help you remember how this piece moves, we will continue to call it a Castle.* □

# The Knight

 s we have learned, the knight was the ultimate fighting machine. In his suit of armor, on his trained and spirited horse, he could overcome any resistance. No foot soldier could withstand his charge. Until the British longbow was introduced, the knight was unconquerable.

Around the eleventh century, a mere seventy knights were able to conquer the entire civilized kingdom of Sicily!

So in chess, the knight's charge cannot be stopped by any piece next to him—he can leap over them on his horse.

*The heavily armored knight on his well-trained horse made a formidable soldier.*

Here is the Knight's move. Notice that it is an L-shaped move: two squares in file (forward or backward) and then one square in rank (to either side). Or, two squares in rank and one in file.

The Knight can move in many directions, and as you can see from this position has eight possible moves!

His move is a surprising one—a leaping, pivoting, L-shaped move—but it can be easily remembered if we think of the actual knight jumping over his enemies on his horse.

The Knight can attack any enemy piece that stands at the end of his move.

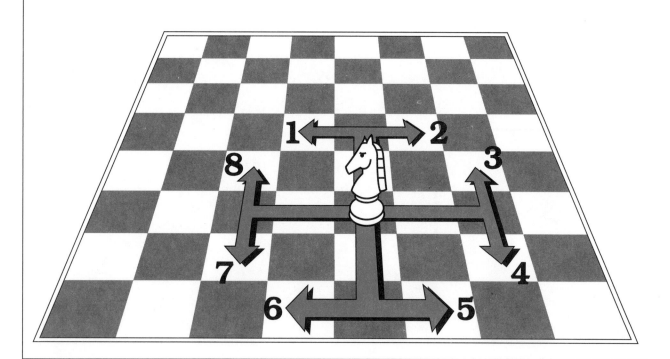

He cannot land in a square of the same color as the square from which he jumps.

In the illustration below, you can see many possible attacks the Knight could make.

Do you also see which attacks would be fatal to him?

**Answer:** The Knight can attack Pawn number 1, Pawn number 2, or Castle number 3 without danger to himself.

But if he attacks Pawn number 4 or Castle number 5, he could be captured on the next move.

Which do you think would be his best move?

**Answer:** The best move is to attack Castle number 3. Why? In chess, we always try to capture the most powerful pieces first. And the Castle is a more important piece than the Pawn.

# The Bishop

The medieval bishop was next to the king and queen in the power he wielded.

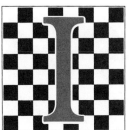 magine the medieval bishop, stately in his long robes and the special hat, called a miter, that set him apart as a member of the clergy. The King and Queen often consulted with the bishop on important decisions—so we say he had the ear of the royalty. Likewise, in chess, he stands next to the King and Queen as though in close contact.

*The bishop's miter, a hat worn only by clergy of his station.*

The Bishop moves on the diagonal, forward or backward as many squares at a time as he wishes.

He can attack any enemy piece that stands on the direct path of his diagonal move.

Below is an illustration showing two Bishops at the start of a game. The Bishop on the left has the choice of either diagonal move, since no piece stands in his way. But the Bishop on the right does not have both diagonals open to him. One diagonal is being blocked by one of his own Pawns. The Pawn must be moved to give the Bishop access to that diagonal.

Except for the Knight, none of the pieces behind the Pawns can be moved until the Pawns are moved.

Here is an illustration to help you learn the Bishop's move. In this situation the Bishop has four possible ways to attack.

Do you see them? Do you see which attacks would be unwise?

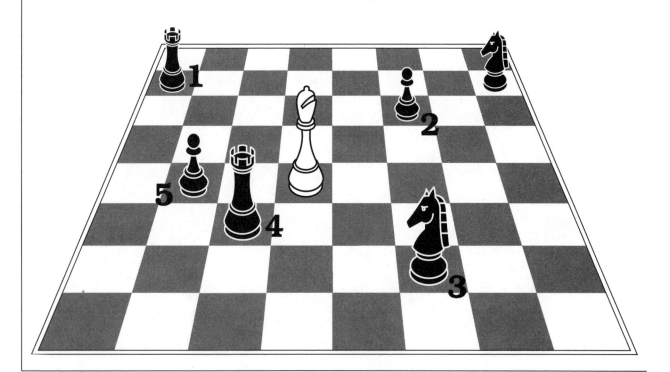

**Answer:** The Bishop can attack Castle number 1 or Knight number 3 without danger to himself. But if he were to attack Pawn number 2, he would be lost to the Knight. If he attacked Castle number 4, he would be lost to Pawn number 5.

■ *For each side, one Bishop remains always on the dark squares, the other always on the light—through the entire game.* □

# The Queen

*The "power behind the throne"—the queen surveys the kingdom from a castle window.*

he medieval Queen had tremendous power over the kingdom. Her moves reflect this, combining the power of the Castle with that of the Bishop. She is the most powerful piece on the board.

She can move forward and backward, from side to side, and on the diagonal—as many open squares as she wishes.

She can capture any enemy piece that stands on these avenues of her attack.

From this illustration we see that she has eight possible directions in which to move and capture!

On the opposite page we see the Queen among her enemies.

How many pieces do you think she could attack? Count them.

Which of these attacks would result in the Queen's capture?

**Answer:** The Queen can attack any of the following Black pieces (five in all) without danger of capture: Either of the Black Bishops, number 5 or 6; Either of the Black Knights, number 4 or 8; or the Black Castle number 3.

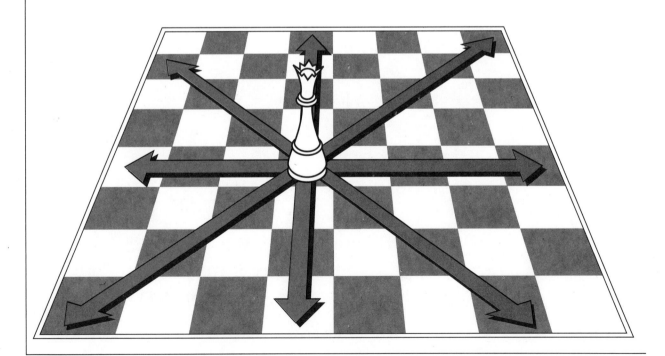

If she attacked Castle number 2, she would in turn be taken by Bishop number 6.

If she attacked Pawn number 1, she would be taken by Knight number 8.

If she attacked Pawn number 7, she would be captured by Castle number 3.

As you can see, it is unwise to attack a piece that is already defended. Always strike the undefended ones!

*The queen's crown, distinguished by its delicate workmanship.*

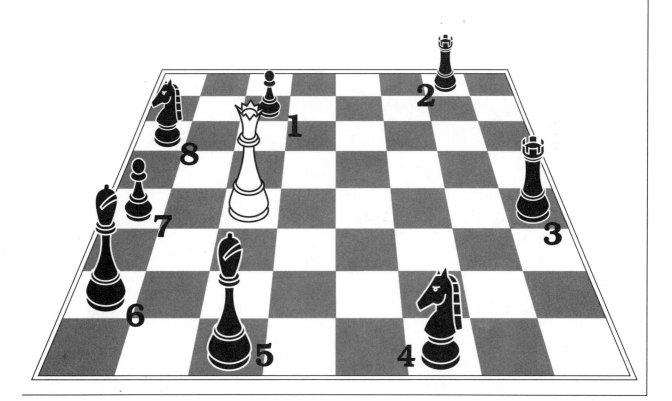

# The King

The king—ruler of the kingdom and the most important piece in chess.

**A**t last the ruler, the reason for chess, the King!

His word was law, and his subjects owed their livelihood and their allegiance to him. Naturally, they would be anxious to see that he survived any battle against an enemy.

So it is in chess. Each piece is moved in an effort to protect its ruler—and capture the enemy's.

Notice that the King moves and attacks in exactly the same way as the Queen, but with kingly deliberation—*only one square at a time.*

The illustration below shows eight possible moves for the King.

When the King is threatened with capture, we use a term that refers only to the King.

This term is the word **check.** It is a warning, and you must say "check" whenever you threaten the enemy King.

When the King is trapped and unable to save himself, we say **checkmate** or **check and mate.**

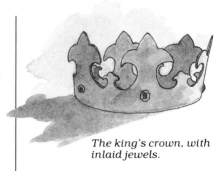

*The king's crown, with inlaid jewels.*

# HOW THE CHESS PIECES MOVE

Here is the White King "in check." That is, he will be captured on the next move unless he can stop the attack.

Can you see what piece threatens him and what he can do about it?

The Black Knight threatens him.

The White King has but one possible move. Do you see it?

Mark the square (lightly with a pencil) where you think he might go. The answer is on the next page.

*The King cannot make a move that places him in check.*

A King can get out of check by one of three means. He moves out of the range of the checking piece, he captures the checking piece, or one of his pieces moves in between him and the enemy threat.

**Answer:** The only possible move for the King is indicated by the arrow.

Obviously in this situation the King's capture is near. When he is finally

"checkmated," he surrenders (or rather the player surrenders), like this.

The King is placed down on the board—and the game is over.

Later on, when we play the game, we will talk more about checking the King.

■ *The word "checkmate" comes from the Persian* shah mat, *meaning "the king is dead."*

Soldiers mourn the loss of their king.

# Castling

There is one special move in chess that involves the King. Its purpose is to remove the King from possible capture.

This move is called **cas-tling** and is done with the King and either one of the Castles.

*The King and the Castle are moved at the same time, in one move.*

Castling is simple: Move the King two spaces to the side, and then move the Castle around the King. This can be done on either side of the King, with either Castle.

This illustration shows how to castle on the Queen's side. Only during castling are two pieces moved at the same time.

**This half of the board is called the QUEEN'S SIDE**

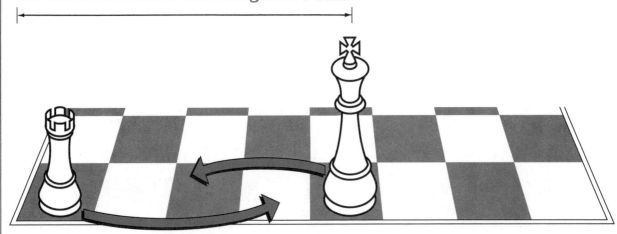

This is castling on the King's side.

You may castle *only* under these conditions:

**1** All the squares between the Castle and King must be open (unoccupied).

**2** The King and the Castle must not have been moved since the beginning of the game.

**3** The King may not be "in check" or have to move through a square threatened by an enemy piece.

*Only once during the game is the King allowed this castling maneuver.*

So much for the basic moves of Chess.

And now we put our new knowledge to the test.

This half is called the KING'S SIDE

# 3 | How to Play

## Blitzkrieg: The Quick Game

*An attacking army zeroes in on the weak spot in the enemy's defense.*

ow that you're familiar with the pieces and how they move, let's play an actual game! You will be the White army.

We'll call this game **blitzkrieg.** This name comes from the German words *blitz,* meaning "lightning," and *krieg,* meaning "war," and was a well-known term in World War II.

A blitzkrieg, or "lightning war," was the tactic of striking the enemy at its weakest point with all possible power, making armies helpless in a very short time.

Before we begin the game, let's take a moment to study the enemy.

In any defense there is one weak spot. A chess defense is no exception.

The Black pawn indicated below is the one weakness in Black's defense. Do you see why?

Study the pieces for a moment and you'll see that this particular Pawn is defended only by the King himself! If the Pawn were captured, only the King could remove the attacker.

White, too, has a weak spot in its defense, but because White has the first move, and consequently the "initiative," the White army need not be concerned.

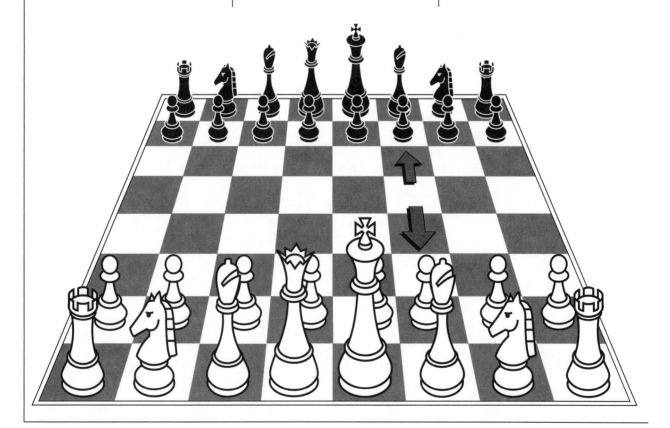

Now we start the game. Remember that we are after the Black King.

We start by moving out with a Pawn (two squares if you like) to the center of the board, like this:

The Pawn is now committed to the battle. And what does that allow you to do on your next move?

The Pawn's move opens up two diagonal avenues. Notice that either the Bishop or the Queen may move to any square on the yellow lines.

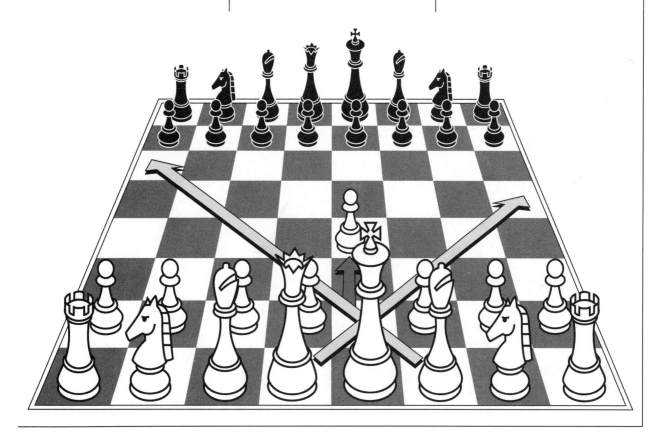

You now have a choice of moving out either of two potentially dangerous pieces!

Black's first move is to block your Pawn with his—a logical and typical countermove.

Now you come out with your Bishop. Do you see that the Bishop now threatens that one weak Pawn?

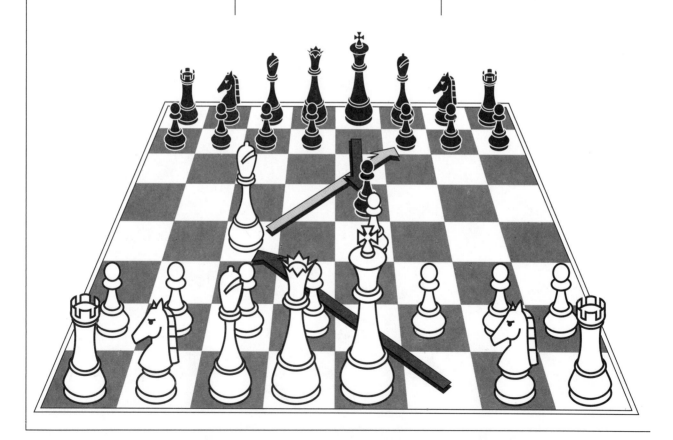

Black again counters by moving his Bishop exactly as you did. It all looks pretty even, doesn't it?

But now, on your move, you bring out your Queen, mounting more pressure on that one weak Pawn.

Suddenly we enter a critical phase of the battle. As in most battles, there is a point when the tide turns and disaster is imminent. This can happen

if a player doesn't have enough reserve troops at the needed moment, or merely doesn't recognize the enemy's strength—or for any one of a score of reasons.

In this game Black simply does not see the threat of your Queen, and comes out with his Knight, like this.

And now you attack with your Queen!

The Black Pawn is taken, and the King is threatened (checked) by your Queen. The King is helpless. He has no place to move to escape the Queen—and he cannot capture the Queen for she is "protected" by your Bishop. A King cannot move into a check position.

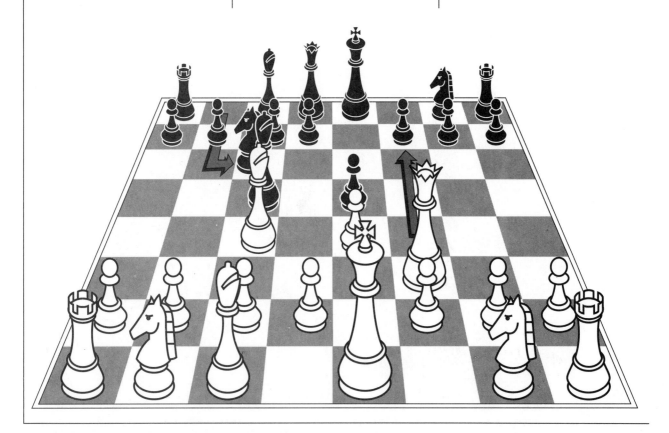

"Check and mate!" Blitz-krieg in only four moves!

Wasn't that a "light-ning" victory? Try this out on a friend, but watch out—your friend might know the blitzkrieg moves, too!

# Beginning the Game

**M**uch of the beginner's knowledge is learned the hard way—lose, lose, and lose again. Through practice, you will develop the skills you need.

While there are many possible strategies in chess, a few basic rules can help you start the game properly.

*Medieval weapons for hand combat and clashes on horseback.*

**1** Try to control the *four center squares* of the chessboard. They get the action, for they are the crossroads of the board.

**2** A good first move, therefore, is to move the Pawn in front of the King (the King's Pawn) two squares forward.

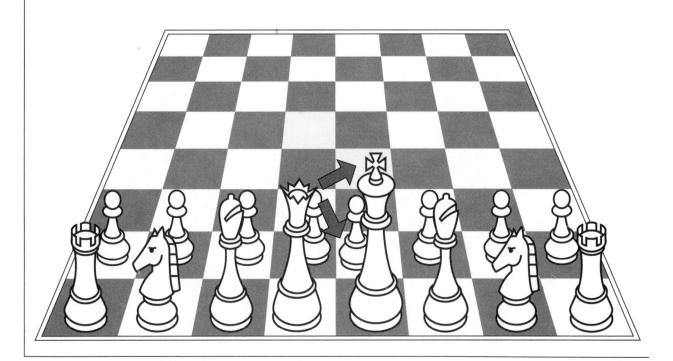

This not only occupies one of those *four center squares* but also opens up diagonal moves for both the Queen and the Bishop.

Moving out the Pawn in front of the Queen (the Queen's Pawn) is also an acceptable first move.

■ *The first 10 or 15 moves of a game are usually called the "opening."* □

**3** Moving out a Knight is also sound, as long as his next move will control one of those *four center squares* (see illustration below).

**4** Try to remember to back up, or protect, each Pawn as soon a possible (see page 25).

For that matter, make it a rule always to back up each piece you move.

This way of playing weaves a strong defense. You know that none of your pieces can be taken without an equal loss to the enemy.

NOT
HERE

HOW TO PLAY

A poor opening move would be to move out the Pawn in front of a Knight or Castle. This sort of move does not control or threaten the center of the board. Nor does it open up paths of attack for the Castles.

**5** Don't keep moving the same piece, unless it is under attack.

If your piece holds or threatens any of those four center squares and it is not in danger, then bring up other pieces to control more of the center squares.

This is always a sound tactic: *When in doubt, bring up more strength—* Pawns, Bishops, Knights—in a slow move toward the opponent's pieces and King.

*The medieval knight—the era's "ultimate fighting machine."*

■ *Nathan Bedford Forrest, a brilliant Southern general in the Civil War, said of victory in battle that it was merely getting there "fustest with the mostest."*

*He was a master at striking where he was least expected. As we play chess with more sophistication, we should bear in mind his famous phrase: "Fustest with the mostest."* □

# Attack and Defense

Once the game is under way and you have done your best to gain control of the center squares, your next series of moves will be to weaken the enemy's defense of his King. How do you do this?

One way is to open a gap in his defensive line through which you can threaten the King, as in the blitzkrieg game. Another way is to capture as many as possible of your opponent's strong pieces—the Queen, Castles, Bishops or Knights—thereby leaving the King defenseless.

*Which one will be his next victim?*

If you can capture his Castle, for example, without losing one of your own, you have gained in stength by weakening your opponent's ability to attack you and to defend himself.

As a good general you must watch the entire board, looking for enemy pieces that are unprotected—and safe to attack—while at the same time making certain that your own pieces are safe.

Sometimes in order to gain an advantage in strength, you might have to give up one of your own pieces. But in doing so, you'll have a surprise in store for your opponent. Chess is a game of surprises, and the idea is to surprise the enemy and not to be taken by surprise yourself.

In the illustration beginning this chapter, you saw a knight charging down on two foot soldiers, and below you have the same situation on the chessboard. If these were your pieces under attack, what would you do?

Remember, watch for surprises!

Let's say you decide to defend Pawn number 2 by moving up Pawn number 3. Now it seems unlikely that the Black Knight would attack Pawn number 2, right? Let's see!

Once one of the Pawns is defended, the obvious victim is the other Pawn. But suppose the Black Knight decides to withhold his attack and instead brings a Castle into the file directly behind him—like this.

Now, when a piece is moved to a certain square, you must quickly determine all the directions that the piece might take on the next move.

Why do you suppose the Black Castle stopped behind his own Knight when obviously he is being blocked by it? Suppose, though, the Knight moves! Then what is threatened?

Watching the entire board, you follow the possible attack of the Castle and find that in that same file is your Queen!

Still that doesn't seem to be a particular danger, so you bring up another Pawn to protect Pawn number 1.

Then the Black Knight moves and captures Pawn number 2. It seems like a silly move at first, for now your Queen can easily attack and remove the Black Castle. Or can she?

As the Knight captures the Pawn, he also checks (threatens) the King! (Re- member, you must watch the entire battlefield.)

Now something must be done—and quickly! Either the King must move out of danger (out of check) or his attacker must be re- moved.

If you study this situa- tion for a moment you might say, "What of it if the King is in check? Didn't I back up that Pawn in the first place?" So you'll just take the Black Knight with your Pawn. What an easy vic- tory—a Pawn lost to cap- ture a Knight.

But now the surprise! The Black Castle sweeps down the board to take your unprotected Queen. What a loss!

You must realize that in chess, as in warfare, it is not just a matter of a strong defense or attack. It is also a matter of timing—*when* to attack.

In this case the Black Knight did not strike until his Castle had been brought into position. Then he attacked with two pieces at once.

Your Pawn was taken even though he was defended; and at the same time that your King was checked, your Queen was also threatened by the Castle. And all this hap-pened with one move of the Knight.

Something had to give! The King had to be saved, and the Queen was lost.

Not the end of the game, to be sure, but neverthe-less a crippling blow. Re-member that a successful attack must have proper strength. And remember, too, WATCH THE ENTIRE BOARD!

# Blitzkrieg Revisited

ow that you know a bit about opening moves, the all-important four center squares, and something about attack and defense, let's play another game.

You've seen how quickly a game can be won. So how about trying the blitzkrieg game again?

This time, however, you'll be up against an opponent with more experience.

You (White) begin and find that each of your moves is met with matching moves until the pieces are situated exactly as in the game on page 59.

A knight on his thundering horse leads the charge into battle.

Now the game becomes exciting, and you wait expectantly for Black to fall into the same fatal trap. Will it happen?

No! Black comes out with his *other* Knight (compare with page 60), blocking your Queen's path! Now what to do?

It seems clear now that your Queen's attack has been stopped, and after

some thought you decide to bring out a Pawn to back up your Bishop and Pawn—a cautious move.

*A medieval knight would carry his sword in this elaborately worked sheath.*

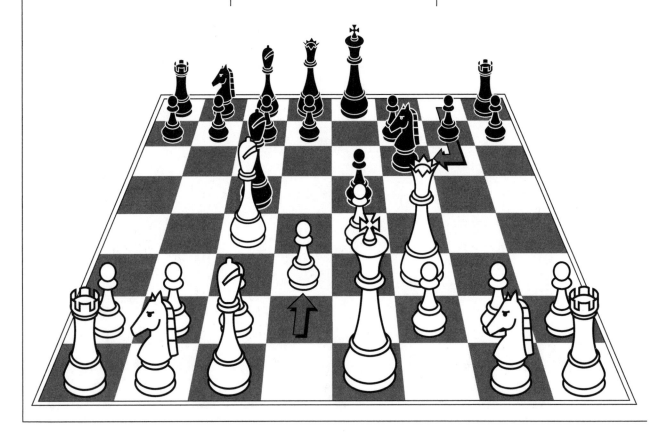

Black, too, seems to be cautious as he moves out a Pawn.

Not certain what to do, you make another cautious Pawn move. At this point, something you can't see has passed from you to your opponent. It is called "initiative."

You kept the initiative during the entire previous game—and won, because at all times you knew just what you wanted to do.

Here you're not sure, and as soon as your enemy sees this, watch out!

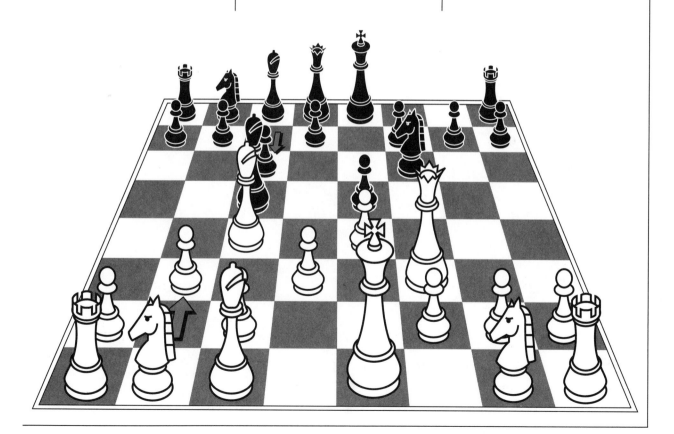

No doubt you know what it's like to walk through a swamp or bog. You can't move very fast, can you?

And when this happens to an attack in battle—when the attack "bogs down"—it is an ideal time for your enemy to strike.

After your second indecisive move Black strikes—a **counterattack!**

Black moves out two squares with a Pawn, simultaneously threatening both your Pawn and your Bishop!

Note, too, that the enemy Pawn is defended three ways (Pawn, Knight, and Queen)!

> ■ *A move that threatens two pieces at once is called a "fork."* □

The Bishop cannot escape, so the Black Pawn *must* be removed.

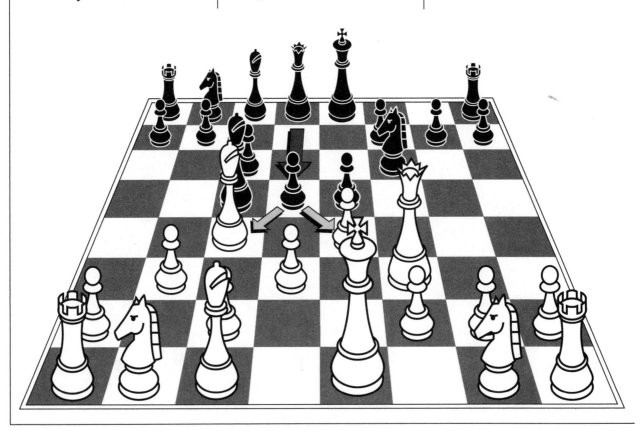

# HOW TO PLAY

Obviously, the best way to dispose of that troublesome Black Pawn is to take him with your Pawn, as shown below, and await Black's next counter.

Notice that even though you have removed one of Black's pieces (the Pawn),

you no longer have the initiative. You're waiting to see what the enemy is planning.

And, of course, the more sophisticated your opponent, the less likely that you'll be able to anticipate his strategy.

Exchanging Pawns would keep the balance of power, but if you could lose a Pawn to capture a Knight or Bishop—without endangering your position—you would be ahead in strength and power.

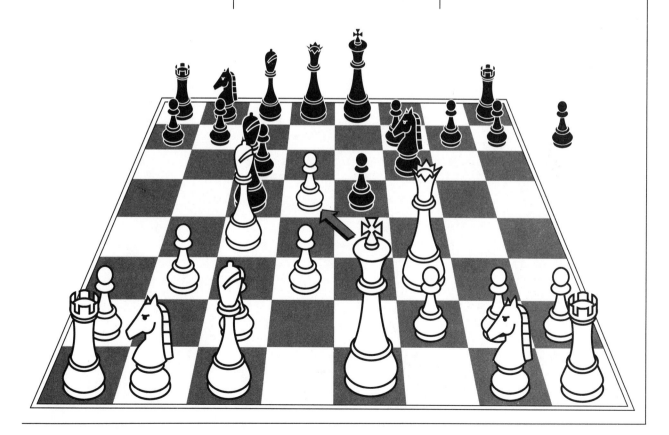

Here Black (the experi-
enced player) does the un-
expected. Instead of using
a Pawn to take your Pawn,
Black opens up an entirely
new area of the battle,
threatening your Queen

with his Bishop! Your
Queen has but one safe
square in which to move.
Each of the other squares
is controlled by a black
piece and the threatening
Bishop is protected by a
Knight.

There is no alternative.
*Your Queen must move to
this position!*
The pressure is ob-
viously on you, and this is
still true after Black moves
his King to a safer posi-
tion and at the same time
brings another strong
piece into play.

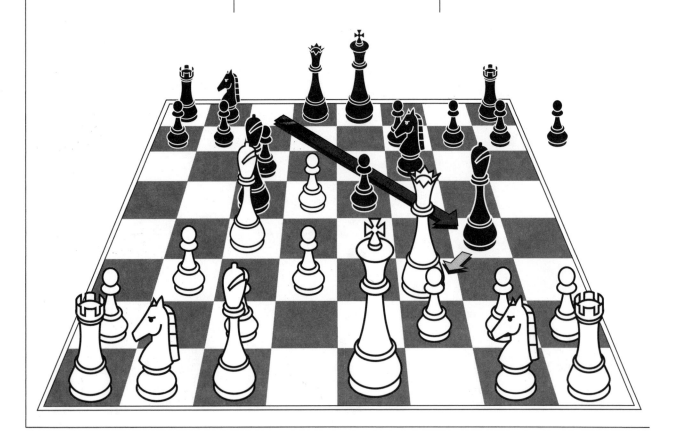

This is done by castling, as shown below.

You're still a bit worried about your Queen, and would like very much to extricate her. And there it is—you spot an undefended Pawn.

A gauntlet, or glove worn with medieval armor, protects the knight's hand.

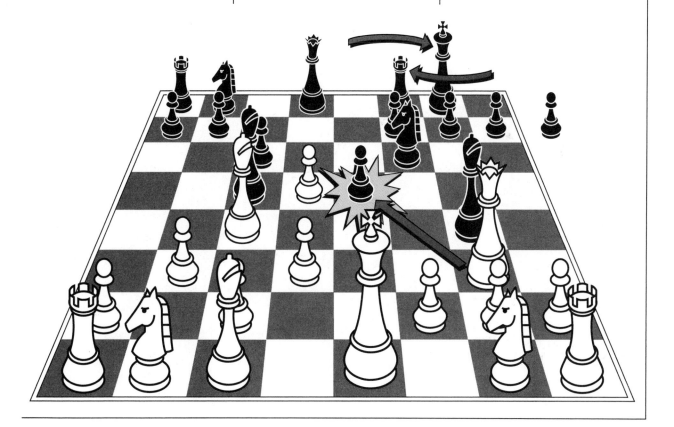

This is probably your most serious mistake since your blitz attack bogged down, for Black merely moves his Castle into your Queen's file!

Now you're in real trouble, for your Queen cannot escape without exposing your King! (And then the game is over!) So you're forced to take the Black Castle.

As you take the Black Castle, you also check the Black King! But this moment of glory may be short-lived.

Note that you've captured *three* Black pieces against *no losses.*

■ *A "gambit" is an opening move in which a piece (usually a pawn) is sacrificed to gain an advantage in position.* □

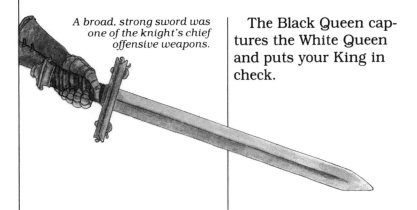

*A broad, strong sword was one of the knight's chief offensive weapons.*

The Black Queen captures the White Queen and puts your King in check.

Either your King must *be moved out of check or the threat must be blocked.* You have several options. But remember: a wrong decision in chess

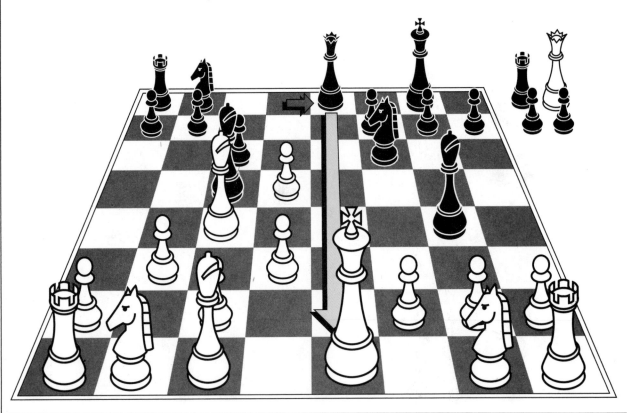

(or in battle) may be fatal. Usually you're not lucky enough to have a second chance.

For example: Suppose you decide to protect your King by blocking the threat with your Knight.

Do you think this is an adequate defense? Let's see.

Unfortunately, it is not, for the Black Queen's attack is backed up by her Bishop!

"Check and mate" and it's over!

Notice that once the counterattack had begun (see page 78) Black never let up the pressure, continually harassing and crowding, so that the strong White pieces could not be used for anything but the defense of the King. Then came the fatal mistake, and the game was over.

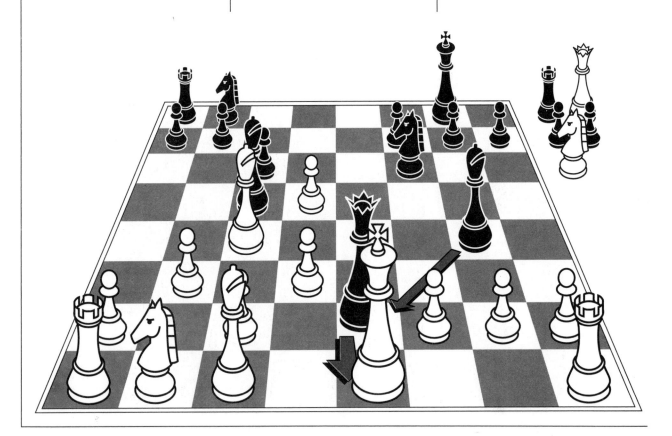

As an exercise, return to page 84 and set up the board exactly as it was when the Black Queen was checking your King.

This time, however, block the Queen's check with your Bishop (rather than the Knight) and from this see how well you can defend and prolong the battle.

This was a much longer game than your blitz attack (see page 55)—and you lost, too! But it was an exciting game, and now you've learned a few surprising tactics.

It's always helpful to analyze our mistakes, regardless. But remember— in chess, mistakes really hurt!

# Ending the Game

o end the game, the enemy King must be put in check by one of your pieces and be unable to get out of it.

There are many ways to end the game. Sometimes your opponent will make a careless mistake—and you must be quick to take full advantage of his error. Your ability to do this comes from being *thoroughly familiar* with the way each piece moves. Remember, in chess there is no luck and no mercy!

*Checkmate—when the king is trapped and unable to save himself—ends the game.*

Here are some thoughts on how to put your opponent's King in check:

**1** Study the King's position, and look for the key square. A **key square** is the one weak spot in the King's defense. (Sometimes there is more than one key square).

The key square in this case would be the square occupied by this Pawn. Do you see why?

**Answer:** All the other pieces are protected (or do not involve the King's defense). This particular Pawn is protected only by the King.

---

91

HOW TO PLAY

If the Black pieces were arranged as shown below, this would be the key square for White to occupy.

Here the Black King is trapped by his own pieces —they are in his way, and he has no escape.

Here the key square is also unprotected, so if a White Queen or Castle could move into that square it would have to be "check and mate."

**2** Once you've decided where the key square is, zero in on it—with all possible strength.

The key square is not always near the King (as in this illustration). Consequently your opponent does not see the danger until it's too late.

**3** Usually it's best to put your most powerful piece, preferably your Queen, into that key square.

**4** Be sure, however, that the key square is properly backed up before you attack! That square can be backed up by several pieces—the more the bet-ter, for sometimes the check does not hold and your opponent is able to escape. The more power that can be brought to bear on a key area, the more quickly the game will be over.

This ability to find the key square comes gradually, as you become more familiar with the way each piece moves.

Right now it's not too easy to see it. However, as you play more and more chess, you'll find it becomes easier and easier. It is also excellent training if you really want to master the game.

■ *The last part of a chess game is called the "endgame."* □

To repeat: The best strategy, after the first few opening moves, is to:

**1** Study the King's position on the board.

**2** Decide which is the key square.

**3** Begin to bring pressure on that area with several pieces. This pressure (and counterpressure by the enemy) builds up slowly. It is usually spoken of as the *middlegame* in chess.

**4** Finally, attack that key square! Attack it with your most powerful piece—if possible, your Queen.

**5** Once the attack is started, keep the King in check with every move, until finally there is no place for him to hide and the game is over. "Check and mate!"

# It's Your Move!

ow you've learned the game of chess. To be sure, you're not a grand master yet, but how well did you swim a year ago? Or bat a ball? These skills have to be developed. And it's the same with chess.

You can play chess all your life—like riding a bicycle, you never forget how.

You've also learned an international language, for chess is played almost everywhere in the world—even against a computer!

Now that you're on your way, you should feel a great sense of accomplishment and be proud of yourself. It's your move!

*The gauntlet has been thrown down and you've accepted the challenge of chess. Let the game begin.*

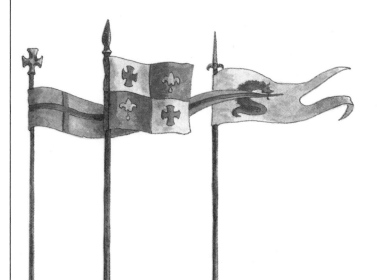

*Now that you're on your way to mastering chess, you may want to learn more about the game. Find out whether your school has a team that you could join. Or contact the U.S. Chess Federation to learn the rules, find a chess club in your area, or enter a scholastic tournament.*

*Their address is:*

*United States Chess Federation*
*186 Route 9W*
*New Windsor, NY 12553*
*(800) 388-KING*

*If you live in Canada, contact:*

*Chess Federaton of Canada*
*2212 Gladwin Crest, Unit E1*
*Ottawa, Ontario K1B 5N1*
*(613) 733-2844*